CONTENTS

Zacchaeus Climbs a Tree 4

A Wonderful Catch of Fish 6

A Young Man Comes Back to Life 8

Jesus Quiets a Storm 10

Jesus Feeds Five Thousand 12

Jesus Walks on Water 14

Jesus Heals Ten Lepers 16

The Good Samaritan 18

The Lost Sheep 20

The Young Man Who Ran Away 22

Jesus' Triumphal Entry Into Jerusalem 24

Jesus at the Temple 26

Jesus Teaches with Stories 28

A Coin for Caesar 30

The Widow's Mite 32

A Woman Anoints Jesus' Feet 34

Judas Takes Thirty Pieces of Silver 36

Preparing for the Last Supper 38

Zacchaeus Climbs a Tree

In the town of Jericho lived a man named Zacchaeus. Nobody liked him because he was a tax collector. He became very rich by making people pay more taxes than they were supposed to. Then he kept the extra money for himself. One day Zacchaeus heard that Jesus was passing through his town. He really wanted to see Jesus. But Zacchaeus was a short man. How would he see over the crowd of people that was always around Jesus? Suddenly he had an idea! He ran down the road and climbed into the branches of a sycamore tree. Now he could see Jesus when He passed by.

Soon Zacchaeus saw a big crowd coming down the road toward him. Then Zacchaeus saw Jesus. But Zacchaeus was surprised when Jesus stopped right under the tree and looked up into the branches.

"Zacchaeus!" Jesus said to him. "Come down quickly. I want to go to your house today." Quickly Zacchaeus climbed down. He was happy to take Jesus to his house.

While Jesus talked with him, something happened to Zacchaeus. Suddenly he felt sad about cheating people. Jesus had changed Zacchaeus' heart. Now Zacchaeus wanted to do good. In fact, he promised to give half of all he owned to the poor. And if he had charged someone too much for taxes, he would give back four times as much.

This made Jesus very happy. It showed that Zacchaeus' life would be different now. Jesus told Zacchaeus, "Your soul was lost. But I came to find lost souls and save them."

CHILDREN'S ALL-TIME FAVORITE BIBLE STORIES
Good Samaritan
A Peter Pan Talking Book

The Good Samaritan and 17 More All-time Favorite Bible Stories from the New Testament

Peter Pan

V. Gilbert Beers and Ronald A. Beers

A Peter Pan Talking Book

Below every story there is a QR code linked to the audio recording of that story. U
your phone or camera to scan the QR code to hear the word-for-word audio.

The Good Samaritan and 17 More All-time Favorite Bible Stories from the New Testament

Copyright ©2020 Inspired Studios, Inc. All rights reserved.

Published by Inspired Studios, Inc, Boynton Beach, Florida 33473

No part of the publication or recording may be reproduced, distributed, or transmitted in any form or by any means, including photocopying, recording, or other electronic or mechanical methods, without the prior written permission of this publisher.

ISBN 978-0-7396-1483-9

A Wonderful Catch of Fish

People loved to listen to Jesus. One day, by the shore of the Sea of Galilee, so many people came to hear Him that they almost pushed Him into the water! Jesus looked around and saw two empty boats by the water's edge. One of them belonged to Simon Peter, a fisher who was mending his nets nearby. Jesus stepped into the boat and asked him to push it out into the water a little ways. Jesus could speak from there.

When Jesus finished teaching the people, He turned to Simon Peter and asked him to row the boat into deeper water. "Then let your nets down, and you will catch lots of fish," Jesus told him.

"Sir," Simon Peter answered Jesus, "we fished all night long. We worked very hard and didn't catch a thing. But we'll try again if you say so."

Simon Peter then threw his nets into the water once again. Suddenly the nets were so full of fish they began to tear. Simon Peter shouted to the other fishers on shore to come help him. Soon two boats were loaded with so many fish they almost sank!

When Simon Peter realized what Jesus had done, he was amazed. So were his partners, James and John. Simon Peter fell to his knees and cried to Jesus, "Sir, please leave us! I am too much of a sinner for You to be around."

Then Jesus calmed Simon Peter. He said, "Don't be afraid. I am making you a fisher of people's souls now." When they reached shore, Simon Peter and his friends left everything and went with Jesus.

A Young Man Comes Back to Life

One day Jesus and His friends went to the little village of Nain. But when they came into the village they saw something sad. There was a line of people, taking the body of a young man to bury.

And there was the young man's mother. She was a widow. Her husband had already died. Now her son, the only one who could take care of her, had died.

Jesus walked toward this funeral. What would He do? Would He say something kind to the woman? Would He try to comfort her? Instead Jesus told her not to weep, and He walked to the body of the young man. Everyone grew quiet now. What would He do?

Jesus pulled aside the sheet covering the young man's face. People began to whisper. Why did He do that?

"Young man," Jesus said. "Get up!" How could Jesus say that to a dead man? What did He expect this dead man to do?

The young man began to rise. The white sheet fell to the ground. The young man stood to his feet. He was alive! "He's alive!" people shouted. "He's alive!" Then the young man hugged his mother.

You can imagine how happy that mother was. You can imagine how many times she thanked Jesus for the wonderful miracle that He had done that day.

Jesus Quiets a Storm

It had been a long, hard day. All morning and all afternoon people had crowded around Jesus. They wanted to hear Him talk about God's wonderful kingdom. They wanted Jesus to heal those who were sick. Jesus loved to be around people. But now He was tired. He needed some rest.

"Let's get in the boat and cross the lake to the other side," Jesus said to His disciples. Jesus went to the back of the boat and soon fell fast asleep.

Before long the wind began to blow hard. Dark clouds formed over the big lake. A big storm was coming.

It swept across the water with great speed. Soon giant waves spilled over the sides of the boat. It looked like the boat would tip over and sink! The disciples were afraid.

Jesus was still in the back of the boat, sound asleep. Some of the disciples rushed over to Him. They woke Him up shouting, "Master! We are about to drown. What can we do?"

Jesus woke up at once. He stood up, faced the terrible storm, and shouted, "Be still!" At once the wind died down and the storm stopped. All was quiet.

Jesus turned to the disciples and said, "Why were you so afraid? Don't you have faith in Me yet?"

The disciples were filled with awe. No ordinary person could do this. "Who can this be?" they asked. "Even the wind and waves obey Him." But they knew He was God's Son.

Jesus Feeds Five Thousand

Jesus climbed to the top of a large hill. Soon over 5,000 people gathered on the hillside around Jesus. Jesus talked with the people all day. They needed to know how to live in a way that pleases God.

Soon it would be dinnertime. Certainly the people were getting hungry. But they didn't want to leave Jesus.

Jesus turned to Philip and said, "Philip, where can we buy some food to feed these people?" Philip couldn't believe what Jesus was asking.

"It would take a fortune to buy enough food to feed all these people," he replied to Jesus. Andrew, Peter's brother, was nearby. He heard Jesus' question.

"There's a young boy here with five loaves of bread and two fish," he said. "But I suppose that won't feed 5,000 people!" The young boy was glad to give his bread and fish to Jesus.

Then Jesus said something that surprised the disciples. "Tell all the people to sit down." Jesus thanked God for the boy's food. Then He began to break off pieces of bread and fish and hand them to His disciples. He told the disciples to pass out the food to all the people. And do you know what? There was enough food for everyone! In fact, there was so much food left over that the scraps filled twelve full baskets.

"This is a great miracle!" the people said. They knew there was something very special about Jesus.

Jesus Walks on the Sea

"Take the boat to the other side of the Sea of Galilee," Jesus told His disciples. Jesus had preached to the crowds all day. Now He needed to rest and pray. He would join them later.

By the time it got dark, the disciples were halfway across the Sea of Galilee. Suddenly a strong wind began to blow, and they became caught in a storm. They rowed hard against the wind and waves, but they couldn't make any progress.

About four o'clock in the morning the disciples saw someone walking on the water right towards them! At first they thought it was a ghost. They screamed in fright.

But it was Jesus, and He quickly called out to comfort them. "Don't be afraid," He told them. "It is I, Jesus."

Then Peter called to Jesus, "If it really is You, let me walk on the water to You."

"All right," Jesus replied. "Come on."

So Peter jumped over the side of the boat and started walking to Jesus on top of the water. But then Peter looked at the high waves and became scared. As he started to sink, he called out to Jesus, "Save me!" Jesus was right there and reached out to take Peter's hand.

Jesus then said, "Peter, why did you doubt Me?" As they climbed into the boat the storm stopped.

The other disciples could hardly believe it all. "You really are God's Son," they exclaimed.

Jesus Heals Ten Lepers

"Unclean! Unclean!" some men shouted. "Lepers! Ten of them!" others whispered. "Stay away from them."

People did stay away from lepers. These were people with a bad disease called leprosy. Others were afraid of catching it. So they stayed away.

But Jesus did not stay away from the ten lepers. He was not afraid.

"Help us!" the ten lepers cried out to Jesus.

"Go to the priests," Jesus told the lepers. "Show them that you are clean."

The lepers knew what Jesus was saying. If they believed Him, they would be clean by the time they got to the priests. Then the priests would tell everyone they were clean. People would not stay away from them any more.

So the lepers ran toward town to do what Jesus said. By the time they reached town their ugly spots were gone. They were clean.

Before long one of the ten came back to Jesus. "Thank You, thank You!" he said. "Thank You for healing me."

"Weren't there ten of you?" Jesus asked. "Where are the other nine?"

Jesus had healed ten men. But only one man remembered to thank Him.

Today, let us remember to thank Jesus for all He has done for us. Let us be like the one thankful man, not like the nine unthankful men.

The Good Samaritan

One day a man asked Jesus an important question. "What does a person have to do to live forever with God in heaven?"

Jesus asked him a question back. "What does the law of Moses say?"

The man thought for a moment and replied, "Love the Lord your God with all your heart, soul, and mind. And love your neighbor like yourself."

Jesus said, "You are right! If you love people like that, you will live forever."

But the man was not satisfied. There were some people he didn't want to love. What would Jesus say about them?

So he asked Jesus, "Who is my neighbor?"

Then Jesus told him a story about a Jewish man who went on a trip. Along the way the man was attacked by robbers. They beat him up and stole all his money.

Then they left him on the road, hurt and bleeding. After a while a Jewish priest came along. When he saw the poor man lying along the road, he passed to the other side and walked on by.

Later a Levite who worked at the Temple passed by. But he, too, ignored the bleeding man.

Then a Samaritan came along. Most Samaritans and Jews did not like each other. But this Samaritan stopped. He put bandages on the man's wounds. Then he put the man on his donkey and took him to the nearest inn.

"Please take care of this poor man until I return," he said. "I will pay whatever it costs."

After Jesus finished his story, the man knew that everyone was his neighbor and that he should help anyone in need.

The Lost Sheep

"Look at Jesus over there," some Pharisees said. They just couldn't understand why Jesus spent so much time with tax collectors and sinners. *They were bad people. Jesus should stay away from them,* the Pharisees thought. Jesus knew what those men were saying about Him. It was time for Jesus to tell them a story that would help them understand why He talked to those people.

Jesus went over to the Pharisees and said, "What if you owned 100 sheep and one of them got lost? Wouldn't you go out looking for that lost sheep? Wouldn't you search and search until you had found him?"

Of course we would, the Pharisees thought to themselves. They wondered what Jesus was trying to tell them.

Jesus continued His story. "Suppose you finally found this lost sheep," He said. "Wouldn't you be happy it had been found? Wouldn't you carry it home and have a great celebration? Wouldn't you be happy that the lost sheep was now safe at home?"

Then Jesus told the meaning of His story. He said, "When one lost sinner is brought back to God there is great joy in heaven. The lost sinner is part of God's family again. There is much happiness in heaven every time this happens."

Suddenly the Pharisees knew why Jesus spent so much time with sinners. He was trying to help them find God. He didn't want them to be lost sinners anymore. The Pharisees knew they should be doing the same thing.

The Young Man Who Ran Away

Two young men lived with their father in a beautiful home. They had everything they needed. But one son grew restless. He wanted to see the world.

One day this young man talked with his father. "You're going to die some day," he said. "You will leave part of your money to me. I want it now."

The father was sad to hear his son say that. But he gave the young man lots of money. Then the young man went away from home.

The young man thought he was rich. He bought lots of expensive things.

Before long the money was gone. He had spent it all.

Then a famine came to that land. He had no money to buy food. But there was no food to buy, even if he had money.

The young man tried to get a job. But the only work he could get was to feed a man's pigs. He was so hungry now that he wanted to eat the pigs' food.

One day the young man realized he had done a foolish thing. So he left for home. He would beg his father to forgive him.

As he came near his house his father saw him and ran to hug him. "We'll have a party!" the father said. "My lost son has been found." The father was so happy to have his son back. He forgave him and brought him back into the family. That's what God does to us when we ask Him.

Jesus' Triumphal Entry into Jerusalem

Jesus and His friends were near Bethany and Bethphage on the Mount of Olives. It was time for Him to go into Jerusalem. Now He would ride in on a donkey. In this way, Jesus would show people He was God's Son.

"Go into this village and you will find a colt tied," Jesus told some friends. "Bring it to Me. If anyone asks, tell him I need it."

The men found the colt. Some people asked what they were doing. They told them Jesus needed it. Then they brought the colt to Jesus. They put clothes on the colt's back and Jesus sat on it.

As Jesus rode toward Jerusalem, people ran out to meet Him. They cut branches and put them on the road where Jesus would ride. Some even put clothes on the road.

"Praise God!" people shouted. "Praise King David's descendant! Praise the one who comes in the name of the Lord."

Of course this stirred excitement in Jerusalem. Some religious leaders were angry. "Tell these people to stop saying such things," they told Jesus.

"If I do, these stones will cry out," Jesus answered.

Jesus rode on the donkey's colt into Jerusalem. Many years before, the prophet Zechariah had said this would happen. "Your king is coming, humble and riding on a donkey," he said. Jesus was greater than a king. He was God's Son.

Jesus at the Temple

When Jesus rode into Jerusalem He went to the temple. People were buying and selling things in the courtyard there. Moneychangers were trading their money for foreign money. People needed the moneychangers' money to buy things in the temple. But these moneychangers cheated people. They charged more for their money than it was worth.

Others were selling doves. These were used in offerings to the Lord.

Jesus began to throw out the people who were selling. He turned over the moneychangers' tables. Their money spilled on the ground.

"My house is a house of prayer," Jesus said. "That is what the Bible says. But you have made it a house of thieves."

The temple leaders saw what Jesus did. They were angry. They wanted to kill Jesus.

Each day Jesus came to the temple. He taught the people about God. The people listened. They wanted to know what Jesus was saying.

The temple leaders could not hurt Jesus now. The people would not let them. They would have to wait.

At night Jesus left Jerusalem and went back to Bethany.

Jesus Teaches with Stories

"Who said You could do what You do?" some leaders asked Jesus one day. "Who said You could teach what You do?"

Jesus knew it was a trap. These people wanted Jesus to say something wrong. If He did, they would be able to kill Him.

What if Jesus said that God told Him to do these things? The leaders would say He claimed to be from God. That was called blasphemy. They could kill Him for that. What if He said someone else told Him to do these things? That wasn't good enough. Only God could tell someone what to do at the temple. No answer would be good enough. What should Jesus do?

"I will answer your question if you answer Mine," Jesus said. "Who told John the Baptist what to do?"

Now the leaders were trapped. If they said "God did," Jesus would ask why they didn't listen to John. If they said "someone else did," the people would be angry. The people thought God told John what to do.

"We don't know," said the leaders.

"Then I will not tell you who said I could do these things," Jesus answered.

Jesus began to teach the people with stories. We call these stories parables. They have two meanings. One is what the story says. The other is what the story tells about God and heaven. Jesus could teach many things through these stories.

A Coin for Caesar

One day some Pharisees and Herodians came to Jesus. They were religious leaders. They hated Jesus and wanted to kill Him. So they tried to trick Him.

"You are an honest man," they said to Jesus. "You teach the way about God truthfully. You are not worried about what people say about You. So tell us honestly. Is it right to pay taxes to Caesar or not?"

Jesus knew what they were doing. It was a mean, wicked trick to hurt Him. If Jesus said they should pay taxes it would make the people angry. These leaders could stir up the people against Him. If He said they should not pay taxes, it would make the Romans angry. The leaders would stir up the Romans against Jesus. What should He do?

"Why are you trying to trick Me?" Jesus asked. "Show Me a coin that you use to pay taxes."

The men found a coin and showed it to Jesus. "Whose picture and name are on this coin?" He asked.

"Caesar's," they answered. Caesar was the Roman emperor. The Romans ruled the land at that time.

"Give Caesar what belongs to Caesar," Jesus said. "Give God what belongs to God."

The men were amazed at what Jesus said. They did not know how to answer Him. So they left Him and went away.

The Widow's Mite

One day Jesus and His friends were in the temple. They were in a place called the treasury, where people gave their offerings. Money boxes were hanging on the wall around the room.

They watched people put money in the money boxes. Rich people dropped in lots of money. Then a poor widow came in. She dropped in two small copper coins, called mites. They were not even worth one cent today.

"Did you see how much the widow gave?" Jesus asked. They had seen how little she had given, not how much.

"That woman gave more than all the others," Jesus said. His friends must have looked surprised. How could Jesus say this? The woman had given only two small coins. Everyone else gave much more.

But Jesus kept on talking to them. "The others put in extra money they did not need," He said. "The poor widow put in all that she had. She needed those two coins for food and clothing."

Now Jesus' friends knew what He meant. It is not how much a person gives. It is how much a person keeps. The other people had given much. But they had kept more. The widow gave very little. But she kept nothing.

A Woman Anoints Jesus' Feet

Jesus was having dinner with Simon the leper. Simon lived in Bethany. This was the same town where Mary, Martha, and Lazarus lived.

While Jesus was eating, a woman came in with a jar of expensive perfumed oil. It was called nard. The woman opened the jar and poured the oil on Jesus while He ate.

The disciples were angry. "What a waste!" they complained. "This could have been sold for much money. We could have given that money to the poor."

Jesus heard what the disciples said. "Leave the woman alone," He said. "She did something beautiful for Me. You will always have poor people with you. But you will not always have Me with you.

"This woman has put the perfumed oil on Me to help Me. She has prepared Me to be buried after I die." People put perfumed oil and spices on dead friends in those days.

Then Jesus said, "When the gospel is preached, the story of this woman will be told everywhere. People will remember what she has done."

This is true, isn't it? Perhaps you have heard a sermon about this woman.

Judas Takes Thirty Pieces of Silver

Judas Iscariot was one of Jesus' twelve special helpers. Judas had been with Jesus for a long time. He had heard Jesus teach and watched His miracles. But he did not truly love Jesus. He loved money more than Jesus.

That is why Judas went to see the chief priests. These people wanted to kill Jesus. Now Judas would help them.

"What will you pay me to betray Jesus?" Judas asked. He was offering to help them capture his friend. He would sell his friend to these men for money.

"Thirty pieces of silver," the men answered. So they counted thirty silver coins and gave them to Judas. They were glad to pay Judas this money. They would pay lots of money to capture Jesus and kill Him. These men were jealous of the things Jesus did. They wanted people to follow them instead of following Jesus.

Judas took the money. He would betray Jesus for thirty silver coins. When he left, he began to look for a time and place to betray Jesus.

Preparing for the Last Supper

The time had come for the Passover, when the lambs were killed for the Passover supper. This was also called the Feast of Unleavened Bread. Jesus asked two of his disciples to get their Passover supper ready. This supper would be their last supper together. We remember it today when we have Communion. Sometimes we call the supper they ate together the Last Supper.

"Will you do this for us?" Jesus asked them.

"Where should we eat?" they asked.

"When you go into Jerusalem, you will meet a man carrying a pitcher of water," Jesus said. "Follow him to the house where he is going. Ask the owner about our room. He will show you a large upstairs room. You will get that room ready for our supper."

The disciples went into Jerusalem. Everything happened the way Jesus said it would. They met a man with a pitcher of water. They followed the man to a house and asked the owner about a room. The owner showed them the room where they would eat the supper together.

The disciples got the Passover supper ready. Now Jesus and His friends could eat it together. Now they would have a pleasant room for the Last Supper.

Collect All 8
Children's All-time Favorite Bible Stories

Noah and the Great Flood

Moses Is Born

David and Goliath

Daniel in the Lion's Den

Jesus Is Born

The Good Samaritan

Jesus Is Raised from the Dead

Paul Sails and Is Shipwrecked

www.ingramcontent.com/pod-product-compliance
Lightning Source LLC
Chambersburg PA
CBHW061800290426
44109CB00030B/2906